Turn My Heart

Turn my heart

❧ A SACRED JOURNEY FROM BROKENNESS TO HEALING

Susan Briehl & Marty Haugen

GIA Publications, Inc.
Chicago

Turn My Heart

Susan Briehl & Marty Haugen

Photography: Doug Beasley
Cover and book design: KantorGroup, Inc.

"Heart Speaks to Heart," exerpted from *Heart Speaks to Heart: Three Prayers to Jesus* by Henri J.M. Nouwen. Copyright © 1989 by Ave Maria Press, PO Box 428, Notre Dame, IN 46556, www.avemariapress.com. Used with permission of the publisher.

"In Blackwater Woods" by Mary Oliver, *American Primitive* © 1992 by Mary Oliver

Psalms of Lament © 1995 Ann Weems. Used By permission of Westminster John Knox Press.

"Go down into the plans of God." Dom Helder Câmara, from *Hoping Against All Hope* © 1984 Orbis Books, New York

"Night Four Songs" from *The Collected Poems of Langston Hughes* by Langston Hughes, Copyright © 1994 by The Estate of Langston Hughes. Used by permission of Alfred A Knopf, a division of Random House, Inc.

"Twelve Songs," Copyright © 1937 and renewed 1965 by W.H. Auden, from *W.H. Auden, The Collected Poems* by W.H.Auden. Used by permission of Random House, Inc.

"God Remembers," Text: Brian Wren, © 1993 Hope Publishing Co., Carol Stream, IL 60188. All rights reserved. Used by permission.

"Bambelela," (original text and melody South African traditional), arrangement © 2002 JL Zwane Memorial Congregation (adapted by M. Muro and M. Stenerick).

G-6136
ISBN: 1-57999-220-X
Copyright © 2003, GIA Publications, Inc.
7404 S. Mason Avenue, Chicago, IL 60638
1.800.GIA.1358 or 708.496.3800
www.giamusic.com

For our fathers —

John Leonard Briehl
1922-2002

Milton S. Haugen
1920-1969

Table of Contents

An Invitation

Tragedy strikes suddenly. Unrelenting loss persistently erodes hope. Loved ones betray us. Those dearest to us suffer and we feel helpless and afraid. We come face-to-face with the worst we can do to one another and to the earth. When grief floods our hearts and despair robs us of hope, how can we begin the journey toward healing and wholeness?

Sometimes, after a season of sorrow, we look back and realize we were on the journey even when we felt we could not move. Sometimes, we need others to point the way or to take our hand and lead us. At other times, the path rises up to meet us and we find ourselves on a long and difficult road we did not choose.

There is no timeline, map, or direct route. The path is unique to each person, community, and situation. We circle back and leap ahead and then, begin again. Just when we feel as if we are standing on more steady ground, a new loss opens an old pain or an old memory inflicts a new wound. Some seasons of grief are long; some wounds so deep the scars always remain. We are changed forever; none of us ever returns to the time before our world fell apart.

However, we do not wander aimlessly. We are pilgrims on a sacred journey, being drawn ever more deeply into the heart of God. Christ comes to us while we are wounded and weeping, angry or confused, crying out for help. The Spirit slowly, persistently, moves within us, comforting, consoling, and turning our hearts toward hope. God works in many and various ways—through medical care, counseling, programs, and the power of forgiveness (both given and received)—until we glimpse the grace of God mending what is broken, planting seeds of promise in the soil of our sorrow, bringing hope and healing from the ashes of our dreams, raising us to new life.

We never travel alone. We walk beside our companions, seen and unseen, clinging to God's promise never to abandon us. Our path is carpeted with the prayers of those who have gone this way before us. Their longing and lament, their silent weeping and songs of hope entwine with ours. We, too, will leave our prayers on the path for the sake of those who will follow. And, when we cannot pray, when we have no words and little faith, God, who enters and shares our suffering in Jesus, sends the Holy Spirit to pray for us "with sighs too deep for words."

For pilgrims, the journey itself is marked by surprising grace. Week after week, God sets a table among us, feeding us with Christ's very presence at the Feast of the Resurrection. When we least expect it, God provides streams of mercy for the thirsty soul, soothing balm for the broken spirit, and manna for the hungry heart.

This book is a gathering of such graces—prayers and psalms, songs and scripture, poems and pictures—ancient and new. Whether you are the one who is weeping or are walking with one who is, we invite you to join us as prayerful pilgrims, attentive to the active presence of God within and around us. May these be for you what they have become for us: resting places on the way and a constellation of stars to illumine the night sky. ❧

Throughout this book, references are made to a companion *Turn My Heart* music collection also available through GIA Publications. For ordering information, please call 1.800.GIA.1358 or visit www.giamusic.com.

The Journey

Wounded, weeping

P. 2

Turning, trusting

Healing, hoping

Wounded, weeping

Even the sparrow finds a home in your presence, O God,

the wren nests safely in your care.

Look upon me with tender love,

for I, your wounded bird, can neither fly

nor sing your praise.

My heart is broken,

my strength is gone,

my helplessness laid bare.

Gather me beneath your wing;

enfold me with your mercy.

Restore in me the image of your love:

Christ, the wounded healer.

Amen

O God, Why Are You Silent?

O God, why are you silent?
I cannot hear your voice;
the proud and strong and violent
all claim you and rejoice.
You promised you would hold me
with tenderness and care.
Draw near, O Love, enfold me
and ease the pain I bear.

Now lost within my grieving,
I fall, and lose my way;
my fragile, faint believing
so swiftly swept away.
O God of pain and sorrow,
my compass and my guide,
I cannot face the morrow
without you by my side.

My hope lies bruised and battered,
my wounded heart is torn;
my spirit spent and shattered
by life's relentless storm.
Will you not bend to hear me—
my cry from deep within?
Have you no word to cheer me
when night is closing in?

Through endless nights of weeping,
through endless days of grief,
my heart is in your keeping,
my comfort, my relief.
Come, share my tears and sadness,
come, suffer in my pain.
O bring me home to gladness,
restore my hope again.

From pain, draw forth compassion,
let wisdom rise from loss.
O take my heart, and fashion
the image of your cross.
Then may I know your healing
through healing that I share,
your grace and love revealing,
your tenderness and care.

MARTY HAUGEN
CD Track 1

How Long, O God,

will you forget me?
How long, O God,
will you hide your face from me?

How much longer must I bear my grief,
and sorrow fill my heart by night and day?
How much longer will my enemies
have the upper hand?

Look at me, O God, and answer me;
light my eyes or I shall sleep in death.
My enemies shall say that I have lost,
and rejoice at my destruction.

But I rely upon your love, O God,
my heart rejoices in your saving help.
I will sing to the God of life
who has been good to me.

PSALM 13

By the rivers of Babylon
we sat down and wept
as we remembered Zion,
our home so far away.

And there we hung our harps
upon the willow trees
as our captors laughed
and called for joyful songs;
for us there is no music in this foreign land,
the song of God no longer ours to sing.

If ever I forget you, O Jerusalem,
let this hand once raised in praise to you go limp;
and let my voice be silenced
if my heart no longer yearns for you
above all earthly joys.

Remember, Lord, the ones who broke us,
brought us low;
Lord, remember those who raped and crushed our home;
how happy they shall be who get to pay them back,
the ones who dash your future on the stones.

PSALM 137, ADAPTED
CD Track 2

Song IX

Stop all the clocks, cut off the telephone,
Prevent the dog from barking with a juicy bone,
Silence the pianos and with muffled drum
Bring out the coffin, let the mourners come.

Let aeroplanes circle moaning overhead
Scribbling on the sky the message He is Dead,
Put crepe bows round the neck of the public doves,
Let the traffic policemen wear black cotton gloves.

He was my North, my South, my East and West,
My working week and Sunday rest,
My noon, my midnight, my talk, my song;
I thought that love would last for ever: I was wrong.

The stars are not wanted now: put out every one;
Pack up the moon and dismantle the sun;
Pour away the ocean and sweep up the wood;
For nothing now can ever come to any good.

W.H. AUDEN

Once We Sang and Danced

Once we sang and danced with gladness,
once delight filled ev'ry breath;
now we sit among the ashes,
all our dreams destroyed by death.

All the willows bow in weeping,
all the rivers rage and moan
as creation joins our pleading:
"God, do not leave us alone."

God, who came to dwell among us,
God, who suffered our disgrace,
from your own heart, grieved and wounded,
come the riches of your grace.

Come, O Christ, among these ashes,
come to wipe our tears away,
death destroy and sorrow banish;
now and always, come and stay.

SUSAN BRIEHL
See endnotes for more information.

Listen, O God, and Answer Me

for I am poor and broken;
enfold and protect me, your faithful one;
save this servant who trusts in you.

I name you my God, show your mercy to me;
I cry out the whole day to you.
Make joyful the heart of your servant,
this heart I raise to you.

Kind and forgiving One,
you are loving to those who call upon you;
listen, then, to my prayer,
hear my cries and my pleadings.

Now, in my time of trouble, I call,
and I know you will answer.
There is no other god like you,
no one can do what you do.

All the nations on earth you have made,
all nations shall bow to your name,
for all your works are wonderful
and you alone are God.

Lead me, O Teacher, in your way,
that I may walk in truth
and worship you
with a heart given to you alone.

PSALM 86:1–11

Night: Four Songs

Night of the two moons

And the seventeen stars,

Night of the day before yesterday

And the day after tomorrow

Night of the four songs unsung:

Sorrow! Sorrow!

Sorrow! Sorrow!

LANGSTON HUGHES

I Cry from the Depths, O God.

Hear me! Hear my voice!
Open your ears and listen
to my pleas for mercy.

If you held our sin against us
who could stand before you?
But your heart, O God, is forgiving,
your compassion fills us with awe.

With all my heart, I wait for God,
I wait in the hope of God's word;
more eagerly than those who watch for the morning,
my whole being waits for the Holy One.

Like those who watch for the morning,
O Israel, wait in hope for God,
whose love never fails,
whose power shall redeem you;
God will set you free
from the bondage of your sin.

PSALM 130

God Remembers (Pain, Joy, Us...)

God remembers pain:
nail by nail, thorn by thorn,
hunger, thirst, and muscles torn.
Time may dull our griefs
and heal our lesser wounds,
but in eternal Love
yesterday is now,
and pain is in the heart of God.

God remembers joy:
touch of love, taste of food,
all our senses know is good.
Love and life flow by
and precious days are gone,
but in eternal Love
every day is now,
and joy is in the heart of God.

God remembers us:
all we were, all we are,
lives within our Lover's care.
Time may dull our minds
and death will take us all,
but in eternal Love
every life is now:
our life is hid with Christ in God.

BRIAN WREN
CD Track 4

I allowed the tears to flow,

tears I had held back so long;

I let them flow as much as they desired,

making them a pillow for my heart,

and my heart found rest on them,

for only you, O God, and no others

could hear my lament.

Turning, trusting

The whole world finds its life in you, O God,

the sun and the moon, the sea and hills;

your creatures look to you for food,

your children seek your face.

Turn to me in steadfast love

and turn my heart toward you,

for you alone can mend and heal;

you alone can save.

Breathe into me your breath of life;

raise me from the dust of death

that I may face the dawn

and praise your holy name,

through Jesus Christ.

Amen

Shepherd Me, O God

When my heart is broken,
when my life is torn,
shepherd me beyond my grief and loss.

When the waves rush o'er me,
when I'm sinking down,
shepherd me beyond the roaring deep.

Through my days of weeping,
through my sleepless nights,
shepherd me within your loving arms.

When my spirit fails me,
when all hope is lost,
shepherd me from death into new life.

Shepherd me, O God,
beyond my wants,
beyond my fears,
from death into life.

Gently you raise me
and heal my weary soul.
You lead me by pathways
of righteousness and truth.
My spirit shall sing
the music of your name.

Though I should wander
the valley of death,
I fear no evil,
for you are at my side,
your rod and your staff—
my comfort and my hope.

You have set me a banquet of love
in the face of hatred,
crowning me with love
beyond my power to hold.

Surely your kindness and mercy follow me
all the days of my life:
I will dwell in the house of my God
forevermore.

PSALM 23, ADAPTED
CD Track 5

In Blackwater Woods

Look, the trees
are turning
their own bodies
into pillars

of light,
are giving off the rich
fragrance of cinnamon
and fulfillment,

the long tapers
of cattails
are bursting and floating away over
the blue shoulders

of the ponds,
and every pond,
no matter what its
name is, is

nameless now.
Every year
everything
I have ever learned

in my lifetime
leads back to this: the fires
and the black river of loss
whose other side

is salvation,
whose meaning
none of us will ever know.
To live in this world

you must be able
to do three things:
to love what is mortal;
to hold it

against your bones knowing
your own life depends on it;
and, when the time comes to let it go,
to let it go.

MARY OLIVER

You, O Holy One,

have been our refuge
in every generation.

Before the mountains rose,
before you brought forth the earth,
from age to age, you are God.

With a word, you return us to dust:
"Return, O children of earth!"
A thousand years to us
are but a day to you,
short as a watch in the night.

You sweep our days away,
they vanish like a dream;
springing up like grass in the morning,
fading and withered by evening.

So teach us the lessons of mortality
that our hearts may learn wisdom.

PSALM 90:1–6, 12

As Swimmers Dare to Face the Sky

As swimmers dare to face the sky
and water bears them solely,
as gliding hawks rest on the air
and air sustains them wholly,
so would I learn to freely fall
into Your deep embraces
and trust no effort ever earns
Your all-surrounding graces.

DENISE LEVERTOV, ADAPTED
See endnotes for more information.

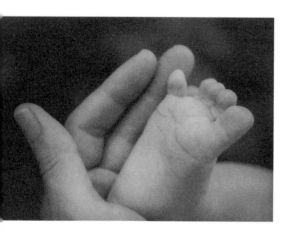

Can a woman forget her nursing child,

or show no compassion

for the child of her womb?

Even these may forget,

yet I will not forget you.

See, I have inscribed you on the palms of my hands.

ISAIAH 49:15–16A, NRSV

Turn, O God!

When will you turn
and show mercy to us, your servants?
Fill us with your love in the morning,
that our hearts may sing all our days.

Give us joy to match the days of our sorrow
and the years that we have suffered.
Let your servants see your saving hand,
show your glory to your children.

May God's sweet favor rest upon us,
may all that we do prosper.
Bless the work of our hands.

PSALM 90:13–17

Once there was a river in the valley
with water clear as crystal
    casting diamonds in the sun.
Now the riverbed is dry and empty,
and no one knows where all the water's gone.

But somewhere from the east
    there come the mem'ries
that weave the morning's sunrise
    with the river's sacrifice.
And those who trust
    the movement of the centuries
can still see the river flow between the times.

Between the times of plenty,
when the water's just a trickle in our lives,
at the time that we must grieve
because the words that we believe
    aren't coming true:
What shall we do between the times?
What shall we do between the times?

Once there was a singer in each person
with a voice as strong as rain and thunder
    carried on the wind.
Now the sounds we make seem so uncertain
that we wonder if we'll ever sing again.

But somewhere from the north
    there come the mem'ries
that whisper on the breeze, across the lakes
    and through the pines,
and those who trust
    the movement of the centuries
can still hear a song to sing
    between the times.

Between the times of plenty,
when the song is just a whisper in our lives,
at the time that we must grieve
because the words that we believe
    aren't coming true:
What shall we do between the times?
What shall we do between the times?

We will look to the west
and behold the holy mountain:
Home to the spirit
    of all the people gone before.
We will put to the test
the faith that we can count on,
All the strength and all the wisdom,
all the hope and all the vision,
all the beauty that still lives in them
    who bid us walk this way once more.

Once there was a road that led to freedom
where kindness walked with truth
    and peace and justice led the way.
Now the people look for one to lead them,
and we weep to see the children go astray,

But somewhere from the south
    there come the mem'ries
of a land of milk and honey
    and the promised rainbow sign.
And those who trust
    the movement of the centuries
can still walk along the road
    between the times.

Between the times of plenty,
when freedom is imprisoned in our lives,
at the time that we must grieve
because the words that we believe
    aren't coming true:
What shall we do between the times?
What shall we do between the times?

RAY MAKEEVER
CD Track 7

In the godforsaken, obscene quicksand of life,

there is a deafening alleluia

rising from the souls of those who weep,

and of those who weep with those who weep.

If you watch, you will see

the hand of God

putting the stars back in their skies

one by one.

ANN WEEMS

Turn My Heart

Turn my heart, O God.
Turn my heart, O God.
Take my pain and brokenness;
shape my life for you.
Come and turn my heart, O God.

From all that leads to death,
to seek the way of life;
from all that leads to sin,
to holiness and grace;
from all despair and grief,
to hope of life renewed:
Come and turn my heart, O God.

O let your Spirit come
and cleanse my inmost heart.
Give back to me the joy
of walking in your way.
O fill me with your grace
that I might sing your praise.
Come and turn my heart, O God.

O bring me home to you,
Most Holy Blessed One,
and let my spirit rest
within your loving heart,
for you alone can raise
my weary soul to life.
Come and turn my heart, O God.

PSALM 51, ADAPTED
CD Track 8

Lord,

when I am famished,

   give me someone who needs food;

when I am thirsty,

   send me someone who needs water;

when I am cold,

   bring me someone to warm;

when I am hurting,

   send me someone to console;

when my cross becomes heavy,

   give me another's cross to share;

when I am poor,

   lead someone needy to me;

when I have no time,

   give me someone to help for a moment;

when I am humiliated,

   give me someone to praise;

when I am discouraged,

   send me someone to encourage;

when I need another's understanding,

   give me someone who needs mine;

when I need someone to take care of me,

   send me someone to care for;

when I dwell upon myself,

   turn my heart toward another.

AUTHOR UNKNOWN

Healing, hoping

O God, you cradle the mountains
and hold the mighty waters
in the hollow of your hand.
You carry the weak in your bosom
and tend each leaf and living thing.

I place myself into your keeping,
my body, my soul, and all that I am,
for you are my help, you are my hope,
you are my highest praise.

Write my name upon your palm,
hold me near your side,
for by your wounds, I am healed,
and in your hands, I am home,
where all will be well.

All will be well in you.
Amen

Healer of Our Every Ill

Healer of our every ill,
light of each tomorrow,
give us peace beyond our fear,
and hope beyond our sorrow.

You who know our fears and sadness,
grace us with your peace and gladness;
Spirit of all comfort, fill our hearts.

You who know each thought and feeling,
teach us all your way of healing;
Spirit of compassion, fill each heart.

MARTY HAUGEN
CD Track 9

$\mathcal{B}$y the tender mercy of our God,

the dawn from on high

will break upon us,

to give light to those who sit in darkness

and in the shadow of death,

to guide our feet in the way of peace.

LUKE 1:78–79, NRSV

ONLY YOU, O GOD

Only you, O God, and you alone,
the broken heart console.
Only you, O God, and you alone,
the wounded world make whole.

O God, our rock and haven,
our stronghold, safe and sure,
though earth be torn and shaken,
in you we stand secure.

You guard us, faithful father,
within your shelt'ring palm;
you nurse us, loving mother,
with milk and healing balm.

We pray, do not abandon
the ones you call your own;
our comfort and companion,
we trust in you alone.

SUSAN BRIEHL
See endnotes for more information.

I Turn My Eyes to the Mountains;

will my help come from there?
No, my help comes from the One
who made the heavens and the earth.

God will not let your foot slip,
the One who guards you never sleeps;
the Holy One, guardian of Israel,
neither slumbers nor sleeps.

God is your protection and shade,
close by your right hand;
nothing will harm you beneath the sun by day,
nor beneath the moon by night.

God will keep you from all evil,
preserving your life;
God will guard you
in every coming and going
now and forevermore.

PSALM 121

Spirit of God,

Life and Life-giver,

Root of all life,

Enlivening Wind,

washing away sin,

anointing each wound,

You are True Life,

alive with Light,

worthy of praise,

awakening the heart

from death

to new life.

HILDEGARD OF BINGEN

Nothing Can Trouble / Nada Te Turbe

Nothing can trouble,

nothing can frighten.

Those who seek God

shall never go wanting.

God alone fills us.

Nada te turbe,

nada te espante.

Quien a Dios tiene

nada le falta.

Solo Dios basta.

JACQUES BERTHIER
CD Track 11

My heart is little, fearful and very timid.

It will always be so.

But you say, "Come to my heart.

My heart is gentle and humble

and very broken like yours.

Do not be afraid.

Come and let your heart find rest in mine

and trust that all will be well."

HENRI J.M. NOUWEN

Bambelela

(Never Give Up)

Bambelela (hold on; never give up).
In times of trouble (never give up).
When you're all alone (never give up).

SOUTH AFRICAN
CD Track 12

Holy, Loving One,

my heart is humble,
my eyes are not restless;
I do not seek things
beyond my grasp.

But I am calm and content,
like a child in its mother's arms.
Like a satisfied child, I am.

O Israel, place your hope in God
this day, and always.

PSALM 131

G o down

into the plans of God.

Go down

deep as you may.

Fear not for your fragility

under that weight of water.

Fear not

for life or limb

sharks attack savagely.

Fear not the power

of treacherous currents under the sea.

Simply, do not be afraid.

Let go. You will be led

like a child whose mother

holds him to her bosom

and against all comers is his shelter.

DOM HELDER CÂMARA

Watch, O Lord

Watch, O Lord,
with all those awake this night.
Watch, O Lord, with all those who weep.
Give your angels and saints
charge over all who sleep.

Tend your ailing ones,
in your love, Lord.
Rest your weary ones,
in your love, Lord.
Bless your dying ones,
in your love, O Lord of all.

Soothe your suffering ones,
heal afflicted ones,
shield your joyous ones,
in your love, O Lord of all.

Hold your grieving ones,
raise your fallen ones,
mend your broken ones,
in your love, O Lord of all.

Guard your little ones,
guide your searching ones,
grant us all your peace,
in your love, O Lord of all.

AUGUSTINE OF HIPPO, ADAPTED
CD Track 13

The Path of Prayer

Prayer is being attentive to God's presence at work within and around us; it awakens, nurtures, and expresses our longing and need for God. Prayer is not a goal; it is a way to God, a journey into God's deep love for us and for the whole world. "Teach us to pray," the disciples begged Jesus, knowing they could not do it alone. We, too, learn to pray from Jesus, who teaches us in scripture and through our mentors, companions, and ancestors in the faith.

Prayer deepens our relationship to God and engages every part of us—heart and mind, eyes and ears, breath and body, our wonder and our wounds. We a light candle, wait in silence, gather around a cross, or sing a song. We hold a rosary, a smooth stone, or the hands of others. We lift our opened palms, trace the sign of the cross on our bodies, bow our heads, close our eyes, or open them wide.

Whenever, wherever we pray we are part of a community, fellow pilgrims on a common journey. We are surrounded by the communion of saints: seekers and teachers, prophets and mystics of every time and place. They join us in raising our praise and petitions to the God of all time and space.

The classic elements of prayer are gathered here—psalms, scripture and the writings of other pilgrims, icons, songs, signs, and gestures. Use one to focus your prayer. Or choose a psalm, a reading, and a song to shape a brief liturgy of prayer. Pray alone or with others. Move around the book as you will or discipline yourself to go slowly, page by page. Listen to the writings and images speaking to each other, then join their conversation. When preparing for common prayer in a small group or a larger community, use or adapt one of the prayer services in this or another book. ⚘

Psalms

The Psalms are the prayerbook of the Bible. From age to age the faithful have found in these prayers the words of their hearts and claimed them as their own. Christians share them with our Jewish brothers and sisters, whose lives gave rise to these songs of longing and lament, thanksgiving and praise. Jesus prayed the Psalms, crying out to God in his distress. When we pray them, we pray along with Jesus, who is our way to God.

The Psalms sing and resonate throughout this book. Their language echoes in the prayers and inspires the poetry, their cadences shape the songs, and their images become visible in the photographs. Psalms are included in each movement of The Journey: psalms of sorrow, psalms of trust, and psalms of hope and healing. Let these few invite you into the whole prayerbook, all 150 psalms, songs for every season in your life of faith. ❧

Suggestions for Prayer with Psalms

You needn't find a psalm that fits your specific mood or situation. Cry out in your distress; sing the sorrow songs. But turn also to psalms of comfort and praise on the bleakest days. Let the light of God's future shine into the nighttime of your fears. Then, when joy dawns, return to the laments. They will remind you of your constant need of God and of God's faithfulness. And they will prepare you for the next time you walk this way, whether leaning on others for strength or supporting those who mourn.

Scripture and Other Writings

When in grief or pain, we often seek answers to the
questions of our wounded hearts: Why? How long? Where
were you! What does this mean? We want clear directions
on what to do. We search the Bible or other books offering
such help, looking for these answers and instructions.
Often, we are disappointed.

The Bible is not a road map or a book of answers; it
is a meeting place. We come to Scripture as pilgrims have
come for centuries, longing for an encounter with Jesus,
God's living and life-giving Word. He comes as one among
us, opening a way to God. The brief biblical passages in
this book are only a few of the promises God makes to us
through the Word. Christ will meet you here, as he meets
every pilgrim seeking him.

We also read the writings of other pilgrims, our mothers
and fathers in the faith. They share their experiences of the

journey, their encounters with Christ, and their stories of God's unfailing love. Gathered here is the wisdom of mystics, poets, martyrs, and teachers from the 4th, 12th, and 20th centuries.

Suggestions for Prayer with Scripture

Quiet your heart and mind. Pray to be open to God's Word. Read a brief scripture passage or biblical story, slowly. Let the words sink into you. Which words, phrases, or promises catch your attention? Repeat them. Linger with them. Rest in them. How does God meet you in these words? How might these words guide, support, comfort, or strengthen you on your journey today? Read the whole passage again. Close with a prayer or write in a journal. You also may read poetry, song lyrics, or other writings in this contemplative way.

ICONS

No human words or works of art can capture or contain God. Yet everything within the realm of the senses can be an icon, a window onto the Holy One, a pathway into the presence of God. Indeed, the whole world is an icon; we glimpse the power and beauty of the Creator in the creation. Christ comes to us, not in heavenly visions, but in what is ordinary and earthly: flowing water, broken bread, pouring wine, and human skin and suffering.

Within this book, Doug Beasley's photographs open to us the wonders of creation and the work of human hands: burning candles, a baby's toes, carved wood, hewn stone, a wounded bird. They make visible the images of God that fill the Psalms: mountain, shelter, healer, rock, and hiding place. They are black and white icons drawing us into the presence of God. ❧

Suggestions for Prayer with Icons

Open the book to one photograph in the morning.
Look at it closely, deeply. Let the image imprint itself
upon your heart. Carry it within you throughout the
day. Close your eyes and call it to mind from time to
time. Let it be a window, a pathway, an abiding place.
Return to the photograph in the evening. Read silently
or aloud the poem or psalm beside it. Or let a song be
the prayer that fills you.

Song

From the first cry of the newborn to the final sigh at the end of life, we sing our lives. We sing lullabies to our babies, ballads to our lovers, songs of comfort and courage around the sick bed, sorrow songs and laments when our hearts are broken, hymns of faith and assurance when we bury our beloved ones. Our lives are a song, sung to God, whose only song is unending love. As the Quaker hymn says, "My life flows on in endless song."

Music moves us in ways words alone cannot. Sung prayer fills our lungs and our bones, pulses with our heartbeat, moves through our limbs. Our tradition teaches us songs for every season, hymns for hearts wounded and being healed. We sing the sacred words and stories of those who have suffered before us, those who have walked the journey from brokenness to healing.

Many of the songs gathered here are hard to sing, so heavy with grief are they. Others console and revive us. Some we cannot sing when our hope is dashed and our joy depleted; we need our fellow pilgrims to sing for us, to us. Their singing holds us up and binds us as one. ❧

Suggestions for Prayer with Song

Let the music wash over you, enter you, becoming your prayer. Sing in solitude or in the silence of your heart, listening for the Spirit who intercedes for us "with cries and groans" too deep for words alone. Sing with others, the living, breathing Body of Christ, praying with one voice to the Holy One.

Silence

"For God alone my soul waits in silence," the Psalmist sings (PSALM 62). Silence often frightens us when we are wounded. We distract ourselves, trying to push down painful memories or hold back the flood of tears. We stay busy, as if control were a sign of healing. We surround ourselves with noise, drowning out the still, small voice of the Spirit.

Though we deny it, we thirst for silence; we yearn to rest beside still waters. Augustine writes that he could not truly mourn the death of his mother until he was quiet and alone in his bed. His journey toward healing began with the tears that flowed from faithful silence. ❀

Suggestions for Prayer with Silence

This book holds a treasure of empty spaces and images of quiet places, invitations into silence. Chose a photograph that quiets your mind and calms your body, or simply close your eyes. Listen to your own rhythmic breathing. With one hand upon your breast, feel your heart beating.

Even though you are surrounded by death or filled with sorrow, you are alive. The Holy Spirit is drawing the beating of your wounded heart into the heartbeat of God's love: Jesus. Rest in God's presence, safe in God's sheltering palm. Let the tears flow. Let the memories rise. Do not be afraid. You are waiting in silence, trusting in God's promise of life made new.

Signs & Gestures

When we pray, we do not transcend our bodies in order to reach a more "spiritual state." Spirit and body cannot be separated. The creation story in Genesis 2 says it this way; we are formed of ordinary garden dirt—*Adam* from the *adamah*, human from the humus—and enlivened with God's own breath. In Jesus, God became human and lived among us. He took on our flesh—a body at once full of divine splendor and fraught with human hunger and thirst, weariness and grief, suffering and death. His life, death, and resurrection reveal how sacred human life is, this life of the beautiful, fragile body.

We honor our bodies and the bodies of others in our prayer. We are respectful and gentle, remembering that we are both broken and beloved children of God. We reach beyond ourselves to touch one another, making visible the love that binds us as one. With tenderness and power, we touch those who are sick or suffering or dying.

Just as God came to us in Jesus, so God comes to us in and with the stuff of daily life: bread and wine, water and oil, words and movements. They are sacramental; by the power of the Holy Spirit, they carry God's own presence, love, mercy, and healing to us.

Breath and heartbeat form the rhythm of prayer. Speech, song, and silence create the melody. Sign and gesture become the dance of the body in prayer, the dance of a community praying together. Even our posture in prayer is part of this dance. Below we explain four ancient practices—the sign of the cross, laying on of hands, anointing with oil, and the sign of peace—and invite you into the blessings of this dance. ❧

MAKING THE SIGN OF THE CROSS

"Receive the cross on your forehead.
It is Christ himself who now strengthens you
with this sign of his love.
Learn to know and follow him."

FROM THE RITE OF CHRISTIAN INITIATION OF ADULTS.

From the time of the apostles until today, Christians have traced a small cross on the foreheads of those being baptized. It is Christ's own signature upon our brow. We no longer belong to the world, or to ourselves, but, as Saint Paul writes, "you belong to Christ and Christ belongs to God," now and forever (I CORINTHIANS 3: 23).

Later, Christians began tracing a larger cross on their own bodies—touching first the forehead, then the breastbone, then one shoulder, and then the other. This sign is both a reminder and an expression of our desire to know Christ more deeply, to follow him more closely, until we are shaped only by his life, his death, his resurrection.

This simple gesture—tracing the cross on our bodies or having another trace it upon our foreheads—draws us back to our baptismal beginnings, to the waters in which we were buried and raised with Christ, born to a new life, and knit into a new community. This sign also draws us into the future, into the many days we are called to follow Jesus. Finally, it carries us to the end: life's end, suffering's end, love's end—Christ. ❧

When do we make the sign of the cross?

We make this sign when we rise in the morning and before we go to sleep, when we begin our prayer alone or with others, when we bless our beloved ones, anoint the sick, soothe the suffering, or commend the dying into God's keeping. We make this sign upon their foreheads in the strong name of the Trinity, the Name in which we were set free, the Name to which we were bound forever in baptism.

"Then little children were being brought to Jesus
in order that he might lay hands on them and pray."

MATTHEW 19:13

The laying on of hands has a rich history in the New Testament. Jesus laid his hands on children and prayed for them and stretched out his hand to heal the sick. The council of elders laid lands on Timothy at the beginning of his ministry, commissioning and empowering him for his work with Saint Paul. Later, Paul reminds Timothy "to rekindle the gift of God that is within [him] through the laying on of hands; for God did not give us a spirit of timidity, but rather a spirit of power and of love and of self-discipline" (II TIMOTHY 1:6).

Many different cultures and religions have understood that simple human touch has curative powers. We know that babies and elderly persons who endure long periods of time without being touched fail to thrive physically and emotionally. The same is true for everyone. Followers of Jesus use touch as he did, to express and evoke God's power and presence.

How do we use the laying on of hands?

One person places one or both hands upon the head of another and prays for God's power and presence. We lay hands on the newly baptized; the one being confirmed, ordained, or commissioned; the wedding couple; the penitent; the sick and the dying. Through our hands, Christ touches and blesses, heals and empowers those in need.

Anointing with Oil

"Are any among you sick?
They should call for the elders of the church
and have them pray over them,
anointing them with oil in the name of the Lord."

JAMES 5:14

An ancient image of the Trinity depicts the Father as
an olive tree, the source of life, the Son as the fruit of the
tree, and the Holy Spirit as the oil, flowing from the tree
and the fruit to the whole world. Early Christians mixed
olive oil and balsam—a plant extract—to make a fragrant
balm used in anointing as a sign of the Spirit's power
to comfort, cleanse, heal, and bless. The Spirit of God,
writes Hildegard of Bingen, is vested in "washing away sin,
anointing every wound" and "awakening the heart from
death to new life" (SEE P. 34).

As Christians have done for centuries, we gather to pray
for and anoint with oil those who are ill or dying. We lay

our hands in blessing upon our frightened child. Caress our beloved with the oil of forgiveness. Anoint a shame-filled sister or anger-bound brother in the name of the Lord. When we are the one in need, we pray to receive with faith the prayers and anointing of others. ❁

How do we anoint with oil?

Set aside ordinary olive oil for anointing. Add a few drops of scented oil so those who are anointed will fill the room with the sweet "aroma of Christ" (2 CORINTHIANS 2:14).
With oil on your thumb, make the sign of the cross upon the person's forehead saying, "In the name of the Father, † Son, and Holy Spirit" or "In the name of † Christ Jesus."
Lay your hands upon the person's head. Pray as you are able.
Trust God's promise to receive your prayers.

SHARING A SIGN OF PEACE

"Jesus came and stood among [the disciples]
and said, 'Peace be with you.'
After he said this, he showed them his hands and side.
Then the disciples rejoiced when they saw the Lord.
Jesus said to them again, 'Peace be with you.'"

JOHN 20:19B–21A

That first Easter evening, the disciples were afraid. They huddled together behind closed doors. Jesus came to them in the midst of their fear, grief, and confusion. He stood among them and spoke peace into their hearts saying, "Peace be with you." He showed them his wounds from the crucifixion, so they would know it was he. Then he breathed his Holy Spirit into this little community. From then until now, Christians have greeted one another with the words of Jesus.

When we share a sign of peace, we declare the presence of the risen Christ to each other. Wherever we are, in times of joy or sorrow, times of lost hope or renewed trust, even when we are estranged from one another, Jesus comes among us, still bearing the wounds of his own suffering and saying, "My peace I leave with you; my peace I give you. I do not give to you as the world gives. Do not let your hearts be troubled, and do not let them be afraid" (JOHN 14:27).

How do we share a sign of peace?

One person says, "Peace be with you," or "The peace of the Lord be with you." The other person replies, "And also with you." Sometimes this greeting is accompanied with a handshake, an embrace, a bowing of the head toward the other, or a kiss. As Saint Paul writes, "Greet one another with a holy kiss" (11 THESSALONIANS 5:26). This kiss of peace is a sign of love among the members of the community and a sign of Christ in their midst.

Prayer Services

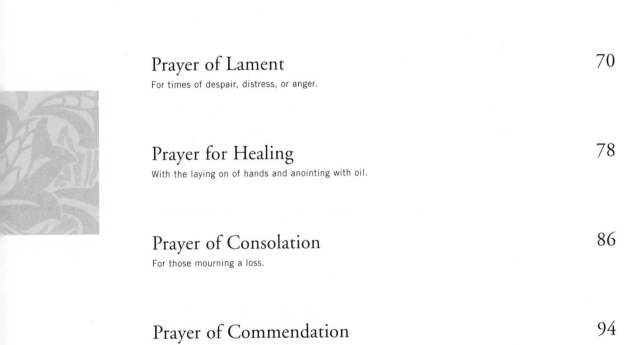

A Simple Way to Pray

Alone or with others.

Entering Prayer

A Place

Choose a place set apart, a place where you feel safe and will not be distracted or interrupted. Sit quietly. Breathe deeply, evenly. Let the thoughts of the day, the worries of the night, the sounds of the space come and go, but do not dwell on them. Wait for the silence to deepen and take root in you. If you come often to this place to pray, you may begin to find God "waiting for you" there. You may choose to light a candle, hold a small cross, or have another sacred symbol near.

An Invitation

As you begin, you may make the sign † of the cross, remembering you are a Child of God.

Pray a simple prayer of invitation as you enter into prayer, such as: "Come, Christ Jesus, come."

or

"Holy God, be with me, for I am _____ *(in trouble, afraid, lonely, weak, sad, or hurting).*"

or

"Speak to me, O God, your servant hears."

LISTENING TO THE WORD

Choose a psalm or a portion of scripture. Read slowly, silently. If you are with others, one person may read it aloud, slowly. Let the words, the images, the pleas, and the promises sink into your heart.

Read it again. What do you hear? What word or promise or phrase speaks to you, seems directed to you? Is this word calling you to confess to God and ask for forgiveness? Is it calling you to praise or thank God? Is it calling you to remember someone else in prayer? Is it bringing hope or truth or comfort to you? Repeat this word or phrase in your mind or on your lips several times.

PRAYING ALONE OR WITH OTHERS

Pray the prayer the Word stirred in your heart. Pray with hands opened, palms uplifted, or choose another prayerful gesture or position.

- If you are drawn to pray for others, pray the name each time you inhale; pray a blessing each time you exhale (e.g. "John, God is with you. John, God is with you," etc. or "John, Jesus loves you. Sarah, Jesus loves you. Douglas, Jesus loves you," etc.).

- If you are stirred to pray for your own needs, with each breath lift your prayer (e.g. "Turn my heart," or "Heal my wounds," or "Remember me," or "Have mercy.").

   ✤ If your prayer is a lament, let it rise and fall with each breath (e.g. "How long, O Lord, how long?" or "Why have you forsaken me?" or "Where were you? Where are you?" or "Rescue me, for I am lost.").

   ✤ If you are with others, each person may voice his or her prayer aloud. The others may join in prayer for the person praying.

   ✤ Whether you cry out from the margins of grief and despair, long to be turned toward trust and hope, or taste anew the sweetness of mercy, do not be afraid; God draws near.

BLESSING AND CLOSING

When your prayer comes to a natural ending, thank God for being near you. Pray the prayer Jesus taught or one of the prayers in this or another book. You may close your prayer as you began, making the sign † of the cross, remembering that you belong to Christ now and always.

A Prayer of Lament

For times of despair, distress, or anger.

    For use in times of crisis or tragedy or grave injustice, when the powers of evil seem to be winning or when God seems far away or silent.

    This prayer service seeks to create a safe place within a community for those gathered to cry out to God in anger, disbelief, pain, or confusion.

    One person serves as the leader. One or more others may read the psalm and the scripture; another may lead the singing.

Gathering

Gather everyone comfortably in a circle. You may place a cross in the midst of those gathered. If appropriate, people may bring signs of the tragedy—newspaper headlines or articles, charred items from a fire, rubble from a natural disaster, belongings or remembrances of those who have died or are lost. When everyone is present, the leader invites all into a time of silent prayer, then says:

LEADER	Peace be with you.
	or
	The Lord be with you.

ALL	**And also with you.**

LEADER	Holy God,
	holy and mighty One,
	holy and immortal One,
	have mercy on us.
	or
	Lord, have mercy,

ALL	**Christ, have mercy.**
	Lord, have mercy.

LISTENING TO THE WORD

The Psalm

READER	Psalm 13

ALTERNATE PSALMS

Psalm 130 (P. 11)

Psalm 137 (P. 6)

How long, O God,
will you forget me?
How long, O God,
will you hide your face from me?

How much longer must I bear my grief,

and sorrow fill my heart by night and day?

How much longer will my enemies

have the upper hand?

Look at me, O God, and answer me.

Light my eyes or I shall sleep in death;

my enemies shall say that I have lost,

and rejoice at my destruction.

But I rely upon your love, O God,

my heart rejoices in your saving help.

I will sing to the God of life

who has been good to me.

MUSICAL SUGGESTIONS

"Why Are You Silent" (P. 140)

"Once We Sang and Danced"
(P. 128)

Song

You may sing a song of lament.

Scripture Reading

ALTERNATE SCRIPTURE PASSAGES

2 Corinthians 4:7–12;
Paul writes, "We are afflicted,
but not crushed."

John 11: 28–35;
Martha's lament to Jesus at the
death of her brother, Lazarus.

READER   A reading from the Gospel of Luke.   Luke 18:1–8

Then Jesus told them a parable about their need to pray
always and not to lose heart. He said, "In a certain city there
was a judge who neither feared God nor had respect for
people. In that city there was a widow who kept coming to
him and saying, 'Grant me justice against my opponent.'
For awhile he refused; but later he said to himself, 'Though

I have no fear of God and no respect for anyone, yet because this widow keeps bothering me, I will grant her justice, so that she will not wear me out by continually coming.'"

And the Lord said, "Listen to what the unjust judge says. And will not God grant justice to his chosen ones who cry to him day and night? Will he delay in helping them? I tell you, he will quickly grant justice to them. And yet, when the Son of Man comes, will he find faith on earth?"

This is the Word of Life.

ALL   **Thanks be to God.**

PRAYER

The leader opens the time of lament with this or another prayer calling on Jesus to be present. Then the leader invites those gathered to name before God their pain, anger, confusion, or sorrow using one of the forms suggested at the end of the prayer.

LEADER   Let us call on Christ, our Advocate,
               to pray with us and for us.

               Draw near to those who call on you, O Jesus,
               for you know our sufferings and our sorrows.
               You withstood the powers of the Evil One;
               stand with us now as we face the powers of evil.

You wept at the tomb of your friend, Lazarus;
weep with us now in our loss and grief.
You cried out to God in your abandonment;
cry out with us as we lift our voices in lament.

ALL   **AMEN.**

If people have brought newspaper or magazine articles—
At the invitation of the leader, people read the headlines or brief portions
of the articles aloud. After each one is read, everyone responds by saying,
"Listen to our cry, O God, listen to our cry," or "How long, O Lord,
how long?"or by singing a Kyrie (SEE P. 123).

If people have brought a sign or artifact of the tragedy, crisis or loss—
At the invitation of the leader, those who are able tell what they have
brought signifies. After each person has spoken, everyone responds by
saying, "Listen to our cry, O God, listen to our cry," or "How long,
O Lord, how long?"or by singing a Kyrie (SEE P. 123).

or

At the invitation of the leader, people cry aloud their laments, giving
voice to their anger, confusion, or grief. After each person speaks,
everyone responds by saying, "Listen to our cry, O God, listen to our
cry," or "How long, O Lord, how long?"or by singing a Kyrie (SEE P. 123).

When the laments have come to a natural close, the leader continues:

LEADER   Let us pray:
Hear our complaints, O God,
answer our cries for help.
In our despair we plead,
trusting you will respond.
Bring an end to death and violence,
and turn to us in mercy,
for you alone are God,
mighty and full of love,
worthy of praise, now and always.
or
You are gracious and merciful, O God,
slow to anger, full of steadfast love.
You are near to those who call,
crying out from their hearts.
Hear our cries and save us,
grant to us life and hope and peace,
through your Son, Jesus Christ.

ALL   **AMEN.**

LEADER   Gathering our prayers into one,
we pray the prayer Jesus taught:

ALL   *[The Lord's Prayer]*

BLESSING

The leader speaks God's blessing upon the whole gathering:

LEADER   May the Holy Trinity, Holy One,

increase our hope,

strengthen our faith,

deepen our love,

✝ and grant us peace.

or

The Lord bless us and keep us.

The Lord's face shine on us.

and be gracious to us.

The Lord look upon us with favor

and ✝ grant us peace.

ALL   AMEN.

MUSICAL SUGGESTIONS

"Only You, O God" (P. 129)

"Amazing Grace" (P. 116)

"Shepherd Me, O God" (P. 132)

Song

A final song may be sung.

A Sign of Peace

The leader may invite those gathered to share Christ's peace with one another.

PRAYER FOR HEALING

With the laying on of hands and anointing with oil.

> *See pages 58–61 of "Signs & Gestures" for an explanation of the laying on of hands and anointing with oil in Christian practice.*

> *Whether you gather at home or elsewhere, you will need a small container of olive oil and a candle. You may use a Bible for additional scripture readings.*

> *To the degree that it is practical, gather everyone around or near the person for whom you are praying. One person serves as the leader. One or more others may read the scripture and the psalm; another may lead the singing.*

GATHERING

When all are ready, the candle is lit and the leader invites them into a time of silent prayer.

Song

You may begin with a simple song or hymn.

MUSICAL SUGGESTIONS

"Only You, O God" (P. 129)

"There Is a Balm in Gilead"
(P. 138)

"Be Still and Know That
I Am God" (P. 117)

Greeting & Prayer

LEADER   Peace be with you.

or

The Lord be with you.

ALL   **And also with you.**

LEADER   Let us pray:

Ever-loving, ever-faithful God,

you are always near to those who call upon you.

As we gather around your servant, *[Name],*

we ask for your healing grace.

Comfort *her/him* with your presence

support *her/him* with your love,

and fill *her/him* with your peace

in Jesus' name.

ALL   **Amen.**

Listening and Responding to the Word

*A simple chant (sung several times by all) may precede or follow
the scripture reading.*

MUSICAL SUGGESTIONS

"Come and Fill Our Hearts"
(P. 118)

"Jesus, Remember Me" (P. 122)

"Kyrie" (P. 123)

"Shepherd Me, O God"
Refrain only (P. 132)

ALTERNATE PSALM

Psalm 86:1–11 (P. 9)

The Psalm

READER   Psalm 23

The Lord is my shepherd,
I want for nothing.

You lay me down in green meadows;
you bring me to rest by calm waters.
In you, my spirit is restored.

You guide me along true pathways;
"Faithful God" is your name.

Even when I walk the dark valley of death
I will not fear.
Evil cannot touch me with you by my side.
Your strong staff is my comfort.

You spread a feast before me,
and my enemies see how you anoint my head
and fill my cup to overflowing.

I know that your goodness and mercy
will abide with me for all my days,
and I will dwell in your house forever.

Scripture

READER   A reading from the Gospel of Mark.   Mark 5:22–24

One of the leaders of the synagogue named Jairus came and, when he saw [Jesus], fell at his feet and begged him repeatedly, "My little daughter is at the point of death. Come and lay your hands on her, so that she may be made well, and live." So [Jesus] went with him.

This is the Word of Life.

ALL   **Thanks be to God.**

Shared Words

The leader may invite the others to reflect upon the scripture readings or to offer words of encouragement to the one receiving the laying on of hands. When all who desire to speak have spoken:

LEADER   Blessed be God,   Psalm 103:2–4
who forgives our sin,
heals every illness,
saves us from death,
enfolds us with tender care,
and crowns us with steadfast love.

ALL   AMEN.

ALTERNATE SCRIPTURE PASSAGES

Matthew 5:2–10;
The beatitudes.

Mark 6:7, 12–13;
The disciples anoint and heal.

Mark 5:25–34;
A woman touches Jesus' hem.

John 5:1b–9;
"Do you want to be well?"

PRAYER

James 5:13–15a

READER   A reading from the Letter of James.

Are any among you suffering? They should pray.

Are any cheerful? They should sing songs of praise.

Are any among you sick? They should call for the elders

     of the church and have them pray over them,

anointing them with oil in the name of the Lord.

The prayer of faith will save the sick,

and the Lord will raise them up.

Laying on of Hands

Depending upon the space and numbers, each person may lay hands upon the person and pray in turn. Or you may form a circle around the individual, linking hands with those laying hands upon her/him, and the leader will pray using these or other words:

LEADER   God bless you and keep you

     and be gracious to you.

     God look upon you with love

     and make you whole.

Anointing

The leader or someone from the group anoints the individual,
making the sign of the cross with oil on the forehead, saying:

LEADER   *[Name]*, beloved child of God,

in baptism you were marked with the cross of † Christ

and sealed with the Holy Spirit

who comes to heal and renew you,

comfort and cleanse you,

strengthen and shield you,

now and forever.

ALL   **AMEN.**

Closing Prayer

LEADER   Let us pray:

Gracious God,

giver of every good and perfect gift,

we praise you for your promise to make us whole.

We thank you for receiving our praise and prayers.

We ask you to fill us with your Spirit

that we might know your peace

and share your love with all in need,

through Christ Jesus.

ALL   **AMEN.**

LEADER   Let us pray the prayer Jesus taught.

ALL   *[The Lord's Prayer]*

Blessing

LEADER   May the Holy Trinity, Holy One,

increase our hope,

strengthen our faith,

deepen our love,

† and grant us peace.

ALL   **AMEN.**

MUSICAL SUGGESTIONS

"Amazing Grace" (P. 116)

"Healer of Our Every Ill" (P. 120)

"Watch, O Lord" (P. 139)

Song

A final song may be sung.

A Sign of Peace

The leader may invite those gathered to share Christ's peace with one another.

PRAYER OF CONSOLATION

For those mourning a loss.

❧ *For use by a small group of persons who mourn the death of a loved one, grieve over a tragedy in the larger world, or console someone who has suffered a loss.*

❧ *If the community is gathering to console one who mourns, you may incorporate the prayer and the laying on of hands from the "Prayer for Healing"* (P. 82) *into this service.*

❧ *One person serves as the leader. One or more others may read the scripture and the psalm; another may lead the singing.*

GATHERING

Gather everyone comfortably close to each other in a circle. You may place a candle (and, if appropriate, mementos of the one(s) whose death you mourn) in the midst of those gathered. When everyone is present, the leader lights the candle and invites all into a time of silent prayer.

MUSICAL SUGGESTIONS

"O God, Our Help in Ages Past"
  (P. 126)

"Only You, O God" (P. 129)

"The King of Love
  My Shepherd Is" (P. 137)

Song

You may begin with a simple song or hymn.

Greeting & Prayer

LEADER   Holy God,

holy and mighty One,

holy and immortal One,

have mercy on us.

or

Peace be with you all.

ALL   **And also with you.**

LEADER   Let us pray:

God of all consolation, source of all mercy,

you weep with those who weep

and comfort all who mourn.

We bring our sorrow to you,

our fear and our confusion.

Hold us in your wide embrace,

console our weary hearts,

and mend our wounded spirits

through Christ Jesus,

whose death reveals your love,

whose rising restores our life.

ALL   **AMEN.**

A simple chant (sung several times by all) may precede or follow the scripture reading.

The Psalm

If used as a litany, the reader invites those gathered to respond to each stanza saying: "We trust in you alone, O God." Alternately this, or another Psalm, may be read without a response.

READER A reading from Psalm 91.

     All who are sheltered by the Most High,
     who abide in the shadow of God,
     say, "My refuge, my fortress, My God!
     My trust is in you alone."

ALL **We trust in you alone, O God.**

READER For God will deliver you from snares and traps,
     God will protect you from deadly plague.
     As a nesting bird covers her young,
     you are safe beneath God's wings.

ALL **We trust in you alone, O God.**

READER You shall fear no terror of the night,
     nor arrows that fly in the day;

No plague that strikes in the dark,

nor disaster in the heat of the day.

ALL   **We trust in you alone, O God.**

READER   God will instruct angels

to guard you everywhere you go.

With their hands they support you,

so you will not stumble on a stone.

ALL   **We trust in you alone, O God.**

Scripture

READER   A reading from the Gospel of John.   John 14:1–3

[Jesus says,] "Do not let your hearts be troubled. Believe in God, believe also in me. In my Father's house there are many dwelling places. If it were not so, would I have told you that I go to prepare a place for you? And if I go and prepare a place for you, I will come again and will take you to myself, so that where I am, there you may be also."

Shared Words

Depending on the occasion, the leader invites those present to offer brief stories and memories of the individual who has died, words of hope and encouragement for the person(s) present and suffering, or reflections upon the tragedy or calamity that has occurred.

Prayer

If the community is gathering to console one who mourns, you may incorporate the prayer and the laying on of hands from the "Prayer for Healing" here (SEE P. 82).

LEADER   Let us pray to the One who is always near to the brokenhearted, saying, Hear our prayer.

When mourning the death of a loved one—

LEADER   Holy God, source of all life,
we give you thanks for our *sister(s) and/or brother(s),*
[Name(s)]
and for our time together in this life.
We commend *her/him/them* into your safekeeping,
trusting in your promise that neither life nor death
can separate us from your love in Christ Jesus.
In your mercy,

ALL   **Hear our prayer.**

For those who mourn—

LEADER   God of all comfort,
draw near to those who mourn, especially *[Name(s)].*
Surround *her/him/them* with faithful friends and companions
and pour out upon *her/him/them* your Holy Spirit.
In your mercy,

ALL   **Hear our prayer.**

LEADER   Merciful God,
           we remember others who suffer in body or spirit,
           naming them before you, silently or aloud.

           Allow time for names.

           Shelter them with your steadfast love and grant them your peace.
           In your mercy,

ALL   **Hear our prayer.**

LEADER   Gracious God, we pray for those throughout the world who suffer
           this day from war or strife, poverty or despair, hunger or disease;
           May our own suffering and sorrow draw us in compassion to them.
           In your mercy,

ALL   **Hear our prayer.**

The leader and others may offer prayers.

LEADER   Eternal God,
           strengthen our faith and increase our hope as we await the day
           when death will end, and crying and pain will be no more.
           Then, with all who have gone before us, we will see you face to face.
           In your mercy,

ALL   **Hear our prayer.**

LEADER   Gathering our prayers into one,

we pray as Jesus taught us:

ALL   *[The Lord's Prayer]*

Blessing

LEADER   May God almighty,

who loves us with an everlasting love,

comfort our hearts by the Holy Spirit

strengthen our faith in Christ Jesus,

now and always.

or

The Lord bless us and keep us

The Lord's face shine on us and be gracious to us.

The Lord look upon us with favor and grant us peace.

ALL   AMEN.

MUSICAL SUGGESTIONS

"Amazing Grace" (P. 116)

"Soft and Tenderly Jesus Is Calling" (P. 134)

"Watch, O Lord" (P. 139)

Song

A final song may be sung.

A Sign of Peace

The leader may invite those gathered to share Christ's peace with one another.

PRAYER OF COMMENDATION

For those to whom death draws near.

GATHERING

As you are able, gather those assembled near the one who is dying.

Greeting and Prayer

LEADER   Remembering Christ's promise never to abandon us,
we gather to commend our *brother/sister, [Name]*,
into God's eternal care and keeping.

Peace be with you.
or
The Lord be with you.

ALL   **And also with you.**

LEADER   Let us pray.
God of all mercy, bless, we pray, your beloved child
[Name]. Comfort *her/him* with your promise of a life
stronger than death, uphold *her/him* with your presence,
and surround *her/him* with all your saints and angels,
through Jesus Christ.

ALL   **AMEN.**

Listening and Responding to the Word

A simple song or hymn may be sung before or following the readings.

MUSICAL SUGGESTIONS

"Only You, O God" (P. 129)

"Shepherd Me, O God" (P. 132)

"The King of Love
My Shepherd Is" (P. 137)

The Psalm

READER   Psalm 139

ALTERNATE PSALMS

Psalm 130 (P. 11)

Psalm 23 (P. 80)

Psalm 131 (P. 37)

Isaiah 49:15–16a (P. 20)

You search me, O God, and you know me.
Whether I sit down or I rise,
you read the thoughts of my heart.
Wherever I travel, whenever I rest,
you search my path and know my ways.
Where can I hide from you?
How can I flee from your presence?
If I climb to the heights, you are there.
If I fall to the depths, you are with me.

If I fly toward the morning
or make my home across the sea,
even there your hand guides me,
your right hand holds me fast.

If I say, "Night will hide me,
the darkness will cover me,"
I find darkness is not dark to you,
for your night is as bright as the day.
In you, darkness and light are one.

ALTERNATE SCRIPTURE PASSAGES

Luke 1:78–79; "By the tender mercy of our God..." (P. 31)

John 14:1–4: "Do not let your hearts be troubled..."

A Reading

LEADER   A reading from Romans.   Romans 8:35, 37–38

Who will separate us from the love of Christ? Will hardship or distress, persecution or hunger, nakedness, danger, or war?

No, in all of these things we are more than conquerors through him who loved us. For I am convinced that neither death nor life, nor angels, nor rulers, nor things in the present, nor anything to come, neither height, nor depths, nor all of creation can separate us from the love of God in Christ Jesus, our Lord.

This is the Word of Life.

ALL   **Thanks be to God.**

Prayer

The Leader begins and ends the prayers. Others may be invited to offer prayers.

LEADER   Let us pray:

Lord God, you have called your servant *[Name]* to ventures of which she/he cannot see the ending, by paths as yet untrodden, through perils unknown. Give *her/him* faith to go out with good courage, not knowing where *she/he* goes,

but only that your hand is leading *her/him* and your love
supporting *her/him*, through Jesus Christ, our Lord.

ALL   AMEN.

When life support is replaced with palliative care
or difficult decisions about care at life's end are made—

LEADER   Holy God, our rock and our refuge, we flee to you in times
of trouble and you shelter us with mercy. We face the limits
of human healing, the imperfection of human knowledge.
Surround us with your infinite wisdom, fill us with your
limitless love, as we entrust to you, the Source of all life,
your child *[Name],* through Christ Jesus.

ALL   AMEN.

Other prayers may be offered here. When the prayers have come to a
natural close:

LEADER   Gathering our prayers into one
we pray as Jesus taught.

ALL   *[The Lord's Prayer]*

Commendation

A song of comfort, peace or rest may be sung. The leader or another
may lay hands upon the head of the dying saying:

MUSICAL SUGGESTIONS

"Amazing Grace" (P. 116)

"Softly and Tenderly Jesus
Is Calling" (P. 134)

LEADER   Beloved Child of God, do not be afraid, God is with you.
          God is with those whom you love. Nothing, neither living
          nor dying, can separate us from the love of God in Christ
          Jesus. Go in peace.

          Into your hands, most gracious God, we commend our
          sister/brother, [Name]. By your tender mercy receive *her/him*
          in death as you have known *her/him* in life: washed in the
          waters of forgiveness, clothed in the righteousness of Christ,
          and sealed with the Holy Spirit.

Blessing
*The Leader may make the sign of the cross upon the forehead of the
dying saying:*

LEADER   In the name of the Father,
          In the name of † the Son,
          In the name of the Holy Spirit:
          One God, now and forever.

ALL   AMEN.

A Sign of Peace
*The leader may invite those gathered to share Christ's peace
with one another.*

Endnotes

Even the sparrow finds a home in your presence, O God

Doug Beasley's photograph evokes images from Psalm 84 of the sparrow homing and the swallow nesting in God's temple. As I prayed, I imagined God's strong and gentle hands holding me and all who are wounded, weak, or vulnerable. The words of Jesus came to me: "Look at the birds of air. God cares for them. Do you think you are of less value?"—*S.B.*

Why Are You Silent? **CD TRACK 1**

For many this tune evokes the wrenching pain of the cross, the deep despair felt when all that one has hoped for is lost. Even though the familiar words of "O Sacred Head" remind us of Christ's ultimate victory over death, the passion and sad beauty of the hymn tune do not diminish the loss that we all have known.

The new text for this hymn grew out of time that I spent with the lament Psalms in scripture, especially Psalms 13, 22, 88, and 102. The writers of the Psalms knew the same despair and sadness that afflicts our lives. In my darkest hours, I came to recognize their honest and heart-felt cries to God as my own.—*M.H.*

Psalm 13

This and all other psalms in this book are our collaborative translation. You may prefer the Psalms as printed in your Bible, prayerbook, or psalter. See the section on the "Psalms" in "The Path of Prayer" (P. 44) for suggestions on how to pray the Psalms.—*M.H. & S.B.*

By the Rivers of Babylon CD TRACK 2

Psalm 137 is the voice of someone who has lost practically everything—homeland, family, and the Temple, the very heart and center of Jewish faith. In despair this refugee can no longer sing the song of faith. When grief, loss and injustice overwhelm us, anger is a natural part of our response. We cannot travel the road from brokenness to healing without naming and expressing our pain. In this Psalm the writer lashes out against the enemies of Israel but, in the end, leaves vengeance to God.—*M.H.*

Stop All the Clocks

Grief can be so complete, so relentless, that we cannot see anything beyond the loss. Love dies. Time stops. The world ends. We cannot imagine a future. Whether our loss is personal or communal, the death of a beloved one or the end of an age of innocence, W. H. Auden speaks the truth we believe, "Nothing now can ever come to any good." To read more poems by Auden, see *W. H. Auden: Collected Poems* (VINTAGE BOOKS: NEW YORK, 1991).—*S.B.*

Once We Sang and Danced

When Lazarus died his sisters, Mary and Martha, called for Jesus, asking him to be with them as they mourned. So too, we ask Jesus to come to the place where we have buried our dreams and to mourn with us and the whole creation, even while we cling to the promise that in Christ, God is making all things new.—*S.B.*

About the Music — Susan crafted her text to fit a hauntingly beautiful Latvian folk tune (commonly called KAS DZIEDAJA). A printed version of this tune with Susan's words is on p. 128; it may be sung to an instrumental version on the *Turn My Heart* CD (TRACK 3). The original Latvian text for this melody refers to the suffering of orphans in a conquered land, comparing them to the Jews in captivity in Babylon. The melody reflects the pain of Psalm 137, a lament sung by those cut off from home and loved ones, and feeling far from God (SEE BY THE RIVERS OF BABYLON P. 6).—*M.H.*

Night: Four Songs

Langston Hughes sings the blues. Low notes. Long night-years. Slow tempo. Four songs. Flatted thirds and sevenths rising from the shared and personal pain of African Americans. The ache enters the bones. The rhythm beats in the heart. The music moves through the soul. The unsung truth is sung: Sorrow. Sorrow. Sorrow. Sorrow. Hughes sings sorrow-songs and much more in *Selected Poems of Langston Hughes* (RANDOM HOUSE: NEW YORK, 1990).—*S.B.*

God Remembers (Pain, Joy, Us...)

CD TRACK 4

Brian Wren gives us this gentle and strong text. It sings of a God who is with us in every moment of life—rejoicing and suffering with us. In dark and lonely moments of suffering and sadness, we can take comfort in knowing that the Holy One is as close as our next breath.

The music drifts between major and minor chords, with unexpected dissonances and resolutions. In the ambiguity of the music, I wanted to mirror Wren's bittersweet words. My friend and colleague, Mary Preus, suggested recording the song as a quiet duet. Even though the words are intended for a congregation to sing, they also reflect an intimacy between God and each of us. Brian Wren's text is taken from *New Beginnings* (HOPE PUBLISHING, CAROL STREAM, IL, 1993).—*M.H.*

I allowed the tears

Augustine, Bishop of Hippo in North Africa (354–430), wrote lovingly of his last days with his mother, Monica. They had shared a vision that lifted them heavenward, where they glimpsed God's wisdom and light. At her death, sorrow flooded him and would have "overflowed in tears," but he silenced "the voice of his heart" and refused to cry, even at her burial. Only later, alone in his bed, did he find solace in weeping for himself and for her, who "had shed so many tears" for him. My translation was taken from his reflection upon these experiences found in chapter 9 of his *Confessions.*—*S.B.*

Turning, Trusting

The whole world finds its life in you, O God

The woman in Doug Beasley's photograph seems both still and strong, as if she were breathing deeply the life-giving breath of the Spirit. Psalm 104 reminds us that every living thing looks to God for food and breath and life. When God turns away, we wither; when God turns toward us, we are renewed. As I looked into the woman's face, I prayed to be turned toward God in trust, even as God is turning toward me in love.—*S.B.*

Shepherd Me, O God Litany   **CD TRACK 5**

"Shepherd Me" came from a place of deep sorrow and the faint, dawning awareness that, in our brokenness, God is able to move us toward a renewed faith and a life marked by compassion and service. The litanic form uses repetition of music and text to bring us back again and again to the truth of our total dependence upon God's life-giving love and mercy.—*M.H.*

In Blackwater Woods

Mary Oliver meditates on the mystery of life: the other side of loss is salvation. Life gives way to death for the sake of life. If we do not love what is mortal and embrace it fiercely, we will never be fully alive. Yet if we refuse to release what we love, even those people, places, and experiences most dear to us, our lives will become a living death. See Oliver's *New and Selected Poems* (BEACON PRESS: BOSTON, 1992).—*S.B.*

As Swimmer's Dare

I adapted "The Avowal," a poem by Denise Levertov, to create this text, which can be sung to "The King of Love." I often struggle to believe in a gracious God, but when my father was dying and I was completely helpless, I found myself in a free-fall, floating into God's embrace, upheld as if by water, as if by air, as if by grace. Levertov's poems on religious themes, *The Stream and the Sapphire*, trace her "own slow movement from agnosticism to Christian faith." Its companion volume, *The Life Around Us*, focuses on ecological themes (NEW DIRECTIONS: NEW YORK, 1997).—*S.B.*

About the Music — There is an instrumental version of "The King of Love" found on the *Turn My Heart* CD (TRACK 6), yoked to another folk tune, "Children of the Heavenly Father" (Susan's adaptation may be sung to the first part of that recorded track). These folk songs—one from the Celtic tradition and one from the Swedish church—have lived in my memory and heart since early childhood. Their sturdy and gentle melodies, honed by the prayer of many generations of believers, uplift and hold us within God's presence, much as Levertov's words.—*M.H.*

Isaiah 49:15-16a

The prophet speaks words of comfort to a people far from their homeland. Even a mother can forsake us, even a father can betray us, he reminds us, but God's love will never fail; God's promises cannot be broken. We are "written" on the palms of God's hands and there we will be held forever.—*S.B.*

Between the Times   CD TRACK 7

Ray Makeever wrote this beautiful ballad "between the times"—after his wife, Judy Essman, had been diagnosed with cancer and before she died. In its honesty and tenderness we can hear the struggle that each of us experiences when facing the most difficult and heart-breaking moments of life. How wonderfully the song reminds us that new hope and faith may be found in remembering and naming the love and faithfulness that extend down through the centuries. Even in the midst of mourning, "there come the memories." Ray's fine song is found in his collection, *Dancing at the Harvest* (AUGSBURG FORTRESS, MINNEAPOLIS, MN, 1997).—*M.H.*

Lament Psalm

Anne Weems lives with an unfinished, unanswered grief for her son, Todd, who died in a car accident when he was twenty-one. On that day, she writes, "the stars fell from my sky." Knowing she never will be comforted fully, she lives where many of us dwell, in that land where anger and alleluias swirl together, where lament and laughter sit side by side in our hearts, and where, if we watch, we can see the hand of God putting the stars back in their skies one by one. Anne Weems dedicates her *Psalms of Lament*, to "Those who weep" and "To those who weep with those who weep" (WESTMINSTER JOHN KNOX PRESS, LOUISVILLE, 1995).—*S.B.*

Turn My Heart

CD TRACK 8

Jewish and Christian tradition suggest that Psalm 51 (from which this song sprung) was first sung by King David in his remorse after his betrayal of Uriah and his affair with Bathsheba (2ND SAMUEL 11-12). It is truly the song of a broken heart yearning for mercy and healing.

I wanted the melody to be as simple as possible, so that those who sing this text might eventually hear only the words. I have found that the simple repetition of short phrases (whether in sung, spoken, or silent prayer) has the power to open us and draw us into a deeper awareness of God's constant presence.—*M.H.*

Lord, When I am Famished

Our sorrow, pain, and fear often turn our entire focus inward, toward our own needs. For a time, this may be necessary, but the journey toward healing eventually turns us outward, sometimes gradually, sometimes abruptly. When, in our suffering, we reach toward others who suffer, we move into a wider world, a world where healing, hope, and wholeness are possible.—*S.B.*

O God, You cradle the mountains

Isaiah's song of comfort rises from these hands: "Who has measured the waters in the hollow of his hand?" (ISAIAH 40:12). The very same God who "gathers the lambs in his arms and carries them in his bosom" (ISAIAH 40:11) says, "Look, I have inscribed you on the palms of my hands" (ISAIAH 49:16). Christ's wounded hands and side welcome me into God's love. And the single, fragile leaf, held in those hands, is sign and seal of resurrection, the life God brings from death.—S.B.

Healer of Our Every Ill Litany   CD TRACK 9

I wrote this song for a healing service at Holden Village, a center for renewal in the Cascades Mountains of Washington State, during the winter of 1985-1986. Since then it has been sung by many communities of many denominations. The text and music reflect my own hope for healing and a prayer for trusting the mysterious movement of God's Spirit.—M.H.

Luke 1:78-79

"Weeping lasts the night, but joy comes in the morning" (PSALM 30:5). The dawning of a new day can turn our hearts toward hope. Old Zechariah sees in the birth of his son, John, the promise of a new age when God's tender mercy will be a light to those who dwell in darkness and a guide for us all on paths of healing and peace. Even now, even among us, this day is dawning in Jesus.—S.B.

Only You, O God

This lyric weaves together images from Psalm 27, a song of trust and a prayer for help attributed to David, and Isaiah 49:14-18 and 66:10-13, songs of comfort to a conquered and exiled people. Our personal losses, needs, and hopes cannot be separated from the hungers of exiles everywhere, the losses and longings of whole peoples, and the wounds of the earth itself. This song turns us again to God, the source of all healing and hope for the brokenhearted and for the wounded world.—*S.B.*

About the music — Susan created these lyrics to be sung with the beloved African-American Spiritual, "There is A Balm in Gilead." A printed version of her words with the tune is on p.129; the words may be sung to an instrumental version on the *Turn My Heart* CD (TRACK 10). The composer is unknown (it was first recorded in 1915). The references to "balm" in the book of Jeremiah are negative (it has no power to heal), but in this spiritual the rich image of oil as a healing balm is a beautiful metaphor for God's love poured out upon those who suffer. The music, as rich and gentle as Susan's words, creates an aural balm for all who seek the healing presence of God.—*M.H.*

The Spirit of God

Hildegard of Bingen (1098-1179) was a woman of visions and poetry. The word of God spoke to her in a rare and beautiful way. My translation tries to capture the essence of this ecstatic song, in which the Holy Spirit is both the source of life and life's sustaining breath. Bingen opens our eyes to see God's Spirit as the One who cleanses, anoints, heals, and wakens us to new life. Barbara Lachman's novel, *The Journal of Hildegard of Bingen* (BELL TOWER: NEW YORK, 1993) is a delightful introduction to this twelfth-century mystic.—*S.B.*

Nothing Can Trouble CD TRACK 11

French composer, Jacques Berthier, created this song for the community of Taizé. A relatively new composition, it hearkens back to ancient Christian roots of meditative prayer and music. Berthier uses a simple repetitive melody and text to draw the seeker into a meditative experience of prayer. The message of God's faithful and constant love resounds in the heart of the singer long after the music has died away. All the music of Taizé is available in North America through GIA Publications.—*M.H.*

My Heart Is Little

Henri Nouwen (1932-1996), a Roman Catholic priest, led many people to deeper prayer through his teaching, writing, and spiritual guidance, but through much of his life, his own heart was lonely and restless. His longing led him to Daybreak, an L'Arche community in Toronto, Canada. Here, living with those the world calls "broken," Nouwen's heart met the wounded heart of Jesus and found its home. He tells the story of this journey in *Heart Speaks to Heart: Three Prayers to Jesus* (AVE MARIA PRESS: NOTRE DAME, 1989). Nouwen's *The Wounded Healer* is a treasure for anyone who would love those who suffer.—*S.B.*

Bambelela

CD TRACK 12

I learned this song from Mairi Munro and Martine Stemerick at a workshop in Birmingham, England. They had heard it sung by the members of the JL Zwane Memorial Congregation, Guguletu, Capetown, South Africa. A Roman Catholic woman from a neighboring church had just shared with this Presbyterian congregation the story of her son, who had recently died of AIDS. After she spoke, the congregation surrounded her and the communion table, singing this song in prayer with and for her. "Bambelela" ("Hold on"): a simple song, a simple message—a powerful and prophetic voice!

The song takes on a greater power when one learns that the JL Zwane Memorial Congregation provides health clinics, support groups, and care projects at the church center. In so much of the music that comes from the oppressed peoples of west and south Africa, from Latin America and from Asia, we hear God's deep identification with the suffering and vulnerable. Their song of hope is lived out in their faith-filled and strong response to God's promises. Because we do not know who composed the song, Mairi and Martine have arranged that the composer's royalties will go to the JL Zwane Memorial Congregation to support them in their ministries.—*M.H.*

Go Down

Dom Helder Câmara (1909-1999), a prophetic Roman Catholic Bishop in Brazil, grew up in the slums of Rio de Janeiro, and chose to live among the poor and to work with them for a more humane future. Amid persecution and death threats on his own life, this small, fragile man writes that hope is "risky loving, trusting others in the dark." Hope is going down, past our pain and our fear, into God's motherly embrace. Câmara's writings include *The Desert is Fertile* and *Hope Against All Hope* (ORBIS: MARYKNOLL, NY, 1984).—*S.B.*

Watch, O Lord CD TRACK 13

St. Augustine, Christian Bishop to North Africa, first prayed this prayer more than 1,600 years ago. As night descends, we invoke and give thanks for God's continuing presence with those who are most vulnerable and with all who watch or weep with them. God's tender care is made known in those who tend the sick, soothe the dying, and comfort those who mourn.

I wanted the music to serve as both lullaby and evening prayer, with a melody that would allow for easy repetition. I chose to retain the word "Lord," even though it is a problematic name for some believers. "Lord" in this context is, for me, the One to whom I give over my life, my safety, my hope. In the end, we all rest in God's hands and depend on God's power to bring us home to healing and hope.—*M.H.*

A Cry of Absence: Reflections for the Winter of the Heart
Martin E. Marty, HarperCollins: New York, NY, 1993.

A Path Through Loss: A Guide to Writing Your Healing & Growth
Nancy Reeves, Northstone Press: Kelowna, British Columbia, Canada, 2001.

All Will Be Well: A Gathering of Healing Prayers
Lynn Klug, ed., Augsburg Fortress: Minneapolis, MN, 1998.

Heart Speaks to Heart: Three Prayers to Jesus
Henri J.M. Nouwen, Ave Maria: Notre Dame, IN, 1989.

Holden Prayer Around the Cross
Susan Briehl and Tom Witt, GIA: Chicago, IL, tbp 2004.

Hoping Against All Hope
Dom Helder Câmara, Translation by Matthew J. O'Connell, Orbis: Maryknoll, NY, 1984.

Lament for a Son
Nicholas Wolterstorff, Eerdmans: Grand Rapids, MI, 1987.

Psalms of Lament
Ann Weems, Westminster John Knox: Louisville, KY, 1995.

Seeing Through Our Tears: Why We Cry, How We Heal
Daniel C. Bagby, Augsburg Fortress: Minneapolis, MN, 1999.

Selected Poems of Langston Hughes
Langston Hughes, Random: New York, NY, 1959.

Without: Poems
Donald Hall, Houghton Mifflin: New York, NY, 1998.

When a Loved One Dies: Meditations for the Journey Through Grief
Philip W. Williams, Augsburg Fortress: Minneapolis, MN, 1995.

Music

This section includes songs that may be used for individual prayer or sung by a small group. We chose both beloved, familiar hymns and newer songs. We know from experience that all this music can be sung without accompaniment. The publisher, GIA, has agreed to allow up to 20 photocopies of these songs to be made without further permission for one-time use by those using the prayer services in this book.

Amazing Grace

Text: St. 1-4, John Newton, 1725-1807; st. 5, attr. to John Rees, fl.1859
Tune: NEW BRITAIN, CM; *Virginia Harmony*, 1831

Be Still and Know That I Am God

Text: Psalm 46:10; John L. Bell
Tune: John L. Bell
© 1989, Iona Community, GIA Publications, Inc., agent

Come and Fill Our Hearts
Confitemini Domino

Come and fill our hearts with your peace.
Con - fi - te - mi - ni   Do - mi - no

You a-lone, O Lord, are ho - ly.
quo - ni - am   bo - nus.
Come and fill our hearts
Con - fi - te - mi - ni

with your peace,
Do - mi - no,
Al - le - lu - ia!
Al - le - lu - ia!

Text: Psalm 137, Give thanks to the Lord for he is good; Taizé Community
Tune: Jacques Berthier (1923–1994)
© 1982, 1991, Les Presses de Taizé, GIA Publications, Inc., agent

Goodness Is Stronger Than Evil

Healer of Our Every Ill

Refrain

Heal - er of our ev - 'ry ill, light of each to -
mor - row, give us peace be - yond our fear, and
hope be - yond our sor - row.

(Last time)

Verses

1. You who know our fears and sad - ness,
2. In the pain and joy be - hold - ing,
3. Give us strength to love each oth - er,
4. You who know each thought and feel - ing,

Grace us with your peace and glad - ness,
How your grace is still un - fold - ing,
Ev - 'ry sis - ter, ev - 'ry broth - er,
Teach us all your way of heal - ing,

Spir - it of all com - fort: fill our
Give us all your vi - sion: God of
Spir - it of all kind - ness: be our
Spir - it of com - pas - sion: fill each

hearts.
love.
guide.
heart.

Text: Marty Haugen
Tune: Marty Haugen
© 1987, GIA Publications, Inc.

Jesus, Remember Me

Je - sus, re - mem-ber me when you come in - to your king - dom. Je - sus, re - mem - ber me when you come in - to your king - dom.

Text: Luke 23:42; Taizé Community
Tune: Jacques Berthier (1923–1994)
© 1981, Les Presses de Taizé, GIA Publications, Inc., agent

Kyrie

Text: *Lord, have mercy.*
Tune: Marty Haugen
© 2001, GIA Publications, Inc.

My Peace

My peace I leave you, my peace I give you: trou-ble not your hearts. My peace I leave you, my peace I give you: be not a-fraid. My

(⌢ Last time)

Text: from John 14, Taizé Community
Tune: Jacques Berthier (1923–1994)
© 1984, Les Presses de Taizé, GIA Publications, Inc., agent

Nothing Can Trouble
Nada Te Turbe

Noth-ing can trou - ble, noth-ing can fright - en.
Na - da te tur - be, na - da te_es - pan - te.

Those who seek God shall nev - er go want - ing. Noth-ing can trou - ble,
Quien a Dios tie - ne na-da le fal - ta. Na - da te tur - be,

noth-ing can fright - en. God a - lone fills us.
na - da te_es - pan - te. So - lo Dios bas - ta.

Text: St. Teresa of Jesus; Taizé Community
Tune: Jacques Berthier (1923–1994)
© 1986, 1991, Les Presses de Taizé, GIA Publications, Inc., agent

125

O God, Our Help in Ages Past

1. O God, our help in a - ges past, Our
2. Un - der the shad - ow of your throne Your
3. Be - fore the hills in or - der stood, Or
4. A thou - sand a - ges in your sight Are
5. Time, like an ev - er - roll - ing stream, Soon
6. O God, our help in a - ges past, Our

hope for years to come, Our shel - ter from the
saints have dwelt se - cure; Suf - fi - cient is your
earth re - ceived its frame, From ev - er - last - ing
like an eve - ning gone, Short as the watch that
bears us all a - way; We fly for - got - ten,
hope for years to come, Still be our guard while

storm - y blast, And our e - ter - nal home.
arm a - lone, And our de - fense is sure.
you are God, To end - less years the same.
ends the night Be - fore the ris - ing sun.
as a dream Dies at the op - 'ning day.
trou - bles last, And our e - ter - nal home.

Text: Psalm 90; Isaac Watts, 1674–1748
Tune: ST. ANNE, CM; attr. to William Croft, 1678–1727

O Lord, Hear My Prayer
The Lord Is My Song

O Lord, hear my prayer, O Lord, hear my prayer:
Alt. text: The Lord is my song, the Lord is my praise:

when I call an-swer me. O Lord, hear my prayer, O
all my hope comes from God. The Lord is my song, the

Lord, hear my prayer: come and lis-ten to me. O
Lord is my praise: God, the well-spring of life. The

(⌒• *Last time*)

Text: Psalm 102; Taizé Community
Tune: Jacques Berthier (1923–1994)

Once We Sang and Danced

1. Once we sang and danced with glad - ness, once de -
2. All the wil - lows bow in weep - ing, all the
3. God, who came to dwell a - mong us, God, who
4. Come, O Christ, a - mong these ash - es, come to

light filled ev - 'ry breath; now we sit a - mong the
riv - ers rage and moan as cre - a - tion joins our
suf - fered our dis - grace, from your own heart, grieved and
wipe our tears a - way, death de - stroy and sor - row

ash - es, all our dreams de - stroyed by death.
plead - ing: "God, do not leave us a - lone."
wound - ed, come the rich - es of your grace.
ban - ish; now and al - ways, come and stay.

Text: Susan Briehl
Tune: KAS DZIEDAJA, Latvian folk song; arr. Marty Haugen
© 2003, GIA Publications, Inc.

Only You, O God

On - ly you, O God, and you a-lone, the
bro - ken heart con - sole. On-ly you, O God, and
you a-lone, the wound - ed world make whole.

1. O God, our rock and ha - ven, our
2. You guard us, faith - ful fa - ther, with -
3. We pray, do not a - ban - don the

strong - hold, safe and sure, though earth be torn and
in your shelt - 'ring palm; you nurse us, lov - ing
ones you call your own; our com - fort and com -

D.C.

sha - ken, in you we stand se - cure.
moth - er, with milk and heal - ing balm.
pan - ion, we trust in you a - lone.

Text: Susan Briehl
Tune: BALM IN GILEAD; trad. Spiritual, arr. Marty Haugen
© 2003, GIA Publicatons, Inc.

Praise God, from Whom All Blessings Flow

Praise God, from whom all bless-ings flow; Praise
him, all crea-tures here be-low; Praise
him a-bove, ye heav'n-ly host; Praise
Fa-ther, Son, and Ho-ly Ghost.

Text: Thomas Ken, (1637–1711)
Tune: OLD HUNDREDTH; Louis Bourgeois (c. 1510–1561)

130

Santo
Holy

¡San - to, san - to, san - to, mi cor - a - zón te a -
Ho - ly, ho - ly, ho - ly, my heart, my heart a -

do - ra! Mi cor - a - zón te sa - be de - cir:
dores you! My heart is glad to say the words:

san - to_e - res Se - ñor.
you are ho - ly, Lord.

Text: Variation on traditional liturgical text
Tune: Traditional Argentine, arr. John L. Bell
© 1990, Iona Community, GIA Publications, Inc., agent

Shepherd Me, O God

Refrain

Shep-herd me, O God, be-yond my wants, be-yond my fears, from death in-to

To verses 1, 2, 3, 5

life.

To verse 4

life.

Verses 1, 2, 3

1. God is my shep-herd, so noth-ing shall I want, I
2. Gent - ly you raise me and heal my wea-ry soul, you
3. Though I should wan - der the val - ley of death, I

rest in the mead-ows of faith-ful-ness and love, I
lead me by path-ways of right-eous-ness and truth, my
fear no e - vil, for you are at my side, your

D.C.

walk by the qui - et wa-ters of peace.
spir - it shall sing the mu - sic of your name.
rod and your staff, my com-fort and my hope.

Verse 4

4. You have set me a ban-quet of love in the face of ha-tred, crown-ing me with love be-yond my pow'r to hold.

D.C.

Verse 5

5. Sure-ly your kind-ness and mer-cy fol-low me all the days of my

poco rit. *a tempo* *To Final Refrain*

life; I will dwell in the house of my God for ev-er-more.

Final Refrain
a bit slower

Shep-herd me, O God, be-yond my wants, be-yond my fears, from

death in-to life.

Text: Psalm 23; Marty Haugen
Music: Marty Haugen
© 1986, GIA Publications, Inc.

Softly and Tenderly Jesus Is Calling

Verses

1. Soft - ly and ten - der - ly   Je - sus is call - ing,
2. Why should we tar - ry when   Je - sus is plead - ing,
3. Time is now fleet - ing, the   mo - ments are pass - ing,
4. O for the won - der - ful   love He has prom - ised,

Call - ing   for   you   and   for   me;
Plead - ing   for   you   and   for   me?
Pass - ing   from   you   and   from   me;
Prom - ised   for   you   and   for   me;

See,   on   the   por - tals   He's   wait - ing   and   watch - ing,
Why should we   lin - ger   and   heed not His   mer - cies,
Shad - ows   are   gath - er - ing,   death - beds   are   com - ing,
Though we have   sinned   He   has   mer - cy   and   par - don,

Watch - ing   for   you   and   for   me.
Mer - cies   for   you   and   for   me?
Com - ing   for   you   and   for   me.
Par - don   for   you   and   for   me.

Refrain

Come home, come home, Ye who are wea-ry, come
home; Ear-nest-ly, ten-der-ly, Je-sus is call-ing—
Call-ing, "O sin-ner, come home!"

Text: Will L. Thompson, 1847–1909
Music: Will L. Thompson, 1847–1909

Take, O Take Me As I Am

Take, O take me as I am; sum-mon out what I shall be; set your seal up-on my heart and live in me.

Text and tune: John L. Bell

The King of Love My Shepherd Is

1. The King of love my shep-herd is, Whose good-ness
2. Where streams of liv-ing wa-ter flow My ran-somed
3. Con-fused and fool-ish oft I strayed, But yet in
4. In death's dark vale I fear no ill With you, dear
5. You spread a ta-ble in my sight; Your sav-ing
6. And so through all the length of days Your good-ness

fails me nev - er; I noth-ing lack if
soul he's lead - ing, And where the ver - dant
love he sought me; And on his shoul - der
Lord, be - side me, Your rod and staff my
grace be - stow - ing; And O what trans - port
fails me nev - er; Good Shep - herd, may I

I am his, And he is mine for ev - er.
pas - tures grow With food ce - les - tial feed - ing.
gent - ly laid, And home, re - joic - ing, brought me.
com - fort still, Your cross be - fore to guide me.
of de - light From your pure chal - ice flow - ing!
sing your praise With - in your house for ev - er.

Text: Psalm 23; Henry W. Baker, 1821–1877, alt.
Tune: ST. COLUMBA, 8 7 8 7; Gaelic

There Is a Balm in Gilead

There is a balm in Gil-e-ad To make the wound-ed whole, There is a balm in Gil-e-ad To heal the sin - sick soul.

1. Some - times I feel dis - cour - aged And think my work's in vain, But then the Ho - ly Spir - it Re - vives my soul a - gain.

2. If you can - not preach like Pe - ter, If you can - not pray like Paul, You can tell the love of Je - sus, And say, "He died for all!"

3. Don't ev - er feel dis - cour - aged, For Je - sus is your friend; And if you lack for knowl - edge He'll ne'er re - fuse to lend.

D.C.

Text: Jeremiah 8:22, African-American spiritual
Tune: BALM IN GILEAD, Irregular; African-American spiritual

Watch, O Lord

Refrain

Watch, O Lord, with all those a-wake this night,

Watch, O Lord, with all those who weep; Give your

an-gels and saints charge o-ver all who sleep.

Verses

Cantor

1. Tend your ail - ing ones:
2. Soothe your suf - f'ring ones:
3. Hold your griev - ing ones:
4. Guard your lit - tle ones:

In your love, Lord;

All

Rest your
Heal af -
Raise your
Guide your

wea - ry ones:
flict - ed ones:
fal - len ones:
search-ing ones:

in your love, Lord;

Bless your
Shield your
Mend your
Grant us

D.C.

dy - ing ones:
joy - ous ones:
bro - ken ones:
all your peace:

in your love, O Lord of all.

Text: A prayer by St. Augustine; adapt. Marty Haugen
Tune: Marty Haugen
© 2003, GIA Publications Inc.

Why Are You Silent?

1. O God, why are you si - lent? I
2. Now lost with - in my griev - ing, I
3. My hope lies bruised and bat - tered, my
4. Through end - less nights of weep - ing, through
5. May pain draw forth com - pas - sion, let

can - not hear your voice. The proud and strong and
fall and lose my way, My frag - ile, faint be -
wound - ed heart is torn; My spir - it spent and
wea - ry days of grief, My heart is in your
wis - dom rise from loss. O take my heart and

vio - lent all claim you and re - joice. You
liev - ing so swift - ly swept a - way. O
shat - tered by life's re - lent - less storm. Will
keep - ing, my com - fort, my re - lief. Come
fash - ion the im - age of your cross. Then

prom - ised you would hold me with ten - der - ness and
God of pain and sor - row, my com - pass and my
you not bend to hear me, my cries from deep with -
share my tears and sad - ness, come suf - fer in my
may I know your heal - ing through heal - ing that I

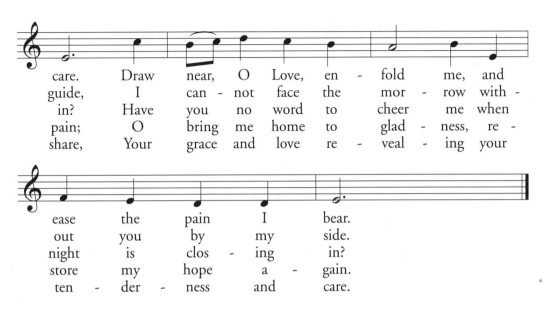

care. Draw near, O Love, en - fold me, and
guide, I can - not face the mor - row with -
in? Have you no word to cheer me when
pain; O bring me home to glad - ness, re -
share, Your grace and love re - veal - ing your

ease the pain I bear.
out you by my side.
night is clos - ing in?
store my hope a - gain.
ten - der - ness and care.

Text: Marty Haugen
Tune: PASSION CHORALE, arr. Marty Haugen
© 2003, GIA Publications, Inc.

World Peace Prayer

Refrain

Lead us from death to life, from false-hood to truth, from des-pair to hope, from fear to trust. Lead us from hate to love, from war to peace; let peace fill our hearts, let peace fill our world, let peace fill our u - ni - verse.

Verses

1. Still all the an - gry cries, still all the an - gry guns,
2. So man - y lone - ly hearts, so man - y bro - ken lives,
3. Let jus - tice ev - er roll, let mer - cy fill the earth,

still now your peo - ple die, earth's sons and daugh-ters.
long - ing for love to break in - to their dark - ness.
let us be - gin to grow in - to your peo - ple.

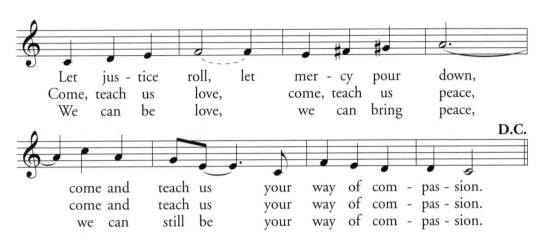

D.C.

Let jus - tice roll, let mer - cy pour down,
Come, teach us love, come, teach us peace,
We can be love, we can bring peace,

come and teach us your way of com - pas - sion.
come and teach us your way of com - pas - sion.
we can still be your way of com - pas - sion.

Refrain Text: Upanishads, Satish Kumar
Verse Text: Marty Haugen
Music: Marty Haugen
© 1985, GIA Publications, Inc.

From The Authors

Grace evokes gratitude like the voice its echo, and we are filled with gratitude. Our spouses, Martin Wells and Linda Haugen, patiently allowed this process to run its long and winding course. Alec Harris and GIA Publications supported this ever-evolving project until the very end. Doug Beasley opened our hearts with his iconic photographs. And Kristy Logan and Dan Kantor of the Kantor Group, blessed us and this book with their wisdom, artistry, and dedication. Such abundant grace calls forth our deepest gratitude.

Susan Briehl & Marty Haugen
LENT III, 2003

About The Photographer

Doug Beasley's photography explores the spiritual aspects of people and place, and that which is considered sacred and ritualized in other cultures as well as our own. To learn more, visit www.vqphoto.com.

About The Designers

KantorGroup is a strategic design consulting firm specializing in elemental/essential communications. The firm emphasizes emotional resonance through clarity, simplicity and potency. To learn more, visit www.kantorgroup.com.

CREATIVE DIRECTION DANIEL KANTOR   **DESIGN AND TYPOGRAPHY** KRISTY LOGAN, SENIOR DESIGNER

Marty Haugen is a composer, workshop presenter, and musician. He lives in Eagan, Minnesota and is a husband and the father of a son and a daughter.

Susan Briehl, a Lutheran pastor and a writer and teacher, lives in Spokane Washington with her husband and their two daughters.